DEAR DEAR

Dear Dear

by Reuben Gelley Newman

WINNER OF THE 2025 LOUISE BOGAN AWARD

Gelley Newman, Reuben
1st edition

ISBN: 978-1-949487-66-4
A Library of Congress Control Number (LCCN) has been requested for this title.

Interior design by Natasha Kane
Cover design by Joel W. Coggins
Editing by David Groff and Samantha Hernandez

Trio House Press, Inc.
Minneapolis
www.triohousepress.org

In memory of Alexander Gelley, 1933–2023

Table of Contents

I

II

I

Self-Portrait as the Cowboy in a Mitski Song

That moment before the song
grooves you, before you know this
is what you want your life to move to
for the next three minutes or hours or days,

that moment before the lover loves you,
before the hope heaves you, before the pop
seethes you & thought eases its synth
drumbeat—churns into the physical,
the thigh-ache & calf-itch & flesh-seize,
before the lover needs you, you're inconsolable,

you're inexorable before they leave you, spinning
through summer sweat you're an aging racetrack
greyhound who scours Genius for Mitski lyrics,
you're the horse named Cold Air, the heart that won't
stop washing itself of love, & why everyone

pores over lyrics as if they were a poem,
& why someone compares her music
to a greyhound, "graceful, but still kind of
sad," I can't say, & why I'm comparing

myself to a cowboy, aching to bridle the tenor
of metaphor, song, & poem, galloping off
on an eighth-note groove, leaping into the do-
mi-ti of my soul, the shatter me, the geyser me,
the *Brokeback Mountain* me, call it

nostalgia, or call it fantasy, or call it
obsess, nonsense, song-sense, song-flesh,
song-gone, song-run, undone, honey-spun, body-none—

I'm no body of music exhaling like a fishless lake,
I'm nobody begging for a kiss—but yes, I know
body, I know its full-bodied wine, it tastes

of lyric, I'm frantic with lyric, giddy-up, Lyric, my canteen's about
to burst, giddy-up, Lyric, wrest my heartbeat, brim my blood—

Jellyfish

for Arthur Russell

I wasn't prepared for your music
when I first heard it: your voice

gliding through consonants
liquid and voiceless,

your cello trembling unlike
a cello, the sound's

edges sanded, weathered
by gales and saltwater,

a jellyfish loping gelatinously
in a vortex of vibrant motion,

and one day I mishear you:
now I find desire imbues it

becomes *now I find desire*
in music. Your mouth kisses

the mic, and we're high
energy, an event horizon,

the boundary around a black hole
beyond which no light can escape,

no words. You're so close
you're unintelligible,

sound swells in the throat's
cavity, vowels vanish

in the murk of mouth and mic
as consonants dissolve

on the tip of the tongue.
I mouth your words;

your words slipstream me.
I wasn't prepared to be stung

by your music—this love.

The Clapping Lights

1.

The name of the next song is "Boy of Your Dreams"—and there I am
visiting the college and there is the boy also visiting, the boy who said
If you're gay and you play cello, you should listen to Arthur Russell,
the boy with turquoise nails and the sparkling red hair of a fox, the boy
I didn't kiss, I don't know why, because I was shy and he was, too,
or the timing wasn't right, or there wasn't enough between us,
and now the music tethers, the sound of whitecaps and deer
in the forest, rabbits' ears and lucky clouds, kaleidoscope of synth
and drum and cello strain, Arthur's voice looping, tripping over itself,
the song on repeat.

2.

Arthur sings, *The name of the next song is* and the song exceeds itself,
restless chords accelerating escape, *California, here I come* from the cornfields
of Iowa, and after the fog of San Francisco, the Buddhist commune and the Golden
Gate Bridge, after cello fugues and ragas had merged in Arthur's ears, he flew
to Manhattan, where the streets glimmered like guitar frets, where he orbited
Ginsberg in '73, where they may have had a fling, where they sang a ballad
about a man searching for profundity in the lights across the Hudson,
a man who thinks the lights are talking to each other before someone sets him
straight, and when I was a kid and we were driving back from the beach I'd spy
the glittering trash heap of suburbia and say *Look! The clapping lights!*
This was in California, and I'm flying to the west coast soon,
and Arthur's alien voice repeats, *This is how we walk on the moon.*

3.

I walk on the moon. All the boys who've never loved me back
come cratering into my arms.

Rave :: aver

Once I fucked a man with *pleasure*
tattooed on his biceps: a sure leap

to joy or jouissance. I was skeptical,
then utterly taken, the slick tape

of caution crumpling over and over
in the mind. I wanted to rove
the straits of desire, to engorge vore

or kink or good boy or yes please,
fever dream. Tell me, was I asleep

in the inner chamber of a keyboard,
fingering the chords, these broad

synth grooves over shoulder, arm, elbow,
tonguing ass and neck, the tattoo below

his groin of a turntable? Answer: could I aver
this desire, dubstep, scene from a rave?

Give

Jasper Johns, Untitled, *Encaustic on linen, 1996*

Give me a map in the shape of a bird.
Give me a thousand amoebas, pulsing.
Give me blue. Give me a blood-stained postcard.
Give me backwards. Give me everything false.
Give me a flock of dimes, a school of pennies.
Give me two boys made of circles & squares
Kissing. Let it never come to an end.

Let it abstract. Let it grow everywhere.
Let it circle & circle & circle.
Let it speck the ramshackle fire escape.
Let it prick, spackle, grow tense & fickle.
Let it past tense & paper clip & gape.
Let it want, let it let, let let unplanned
Kissing. Let it never come to an end.

Smear in the Shape of a Crescent Moon // (Un)faithful Poem Containing White Lies Purely for the Sake of Narrative

with Lorde and Vivaldi

The acid residue
of burnout like coffee left
in a thermos for three days. Wondering
if your boyfriend gave your necklaces
back when you left them, longingly,
at his place. Remembering that both you
and he forgot them. You forget your keys
today, you'll have to ask the neighbor to buzz
you into your apartment. What'd it be like
to buzz out of the beat of life for a minute,
to elide the algo rhythm. Instagram brings you
reels of bassoonists, all the jokes about the word
when translated into German. You play Vivaldi's
Fagottkonzerte, you exalt faggotry and frolicking.
One summer you streamed *Melodrama*
on repeat, wanting to seem hip;
come this fall you've still only played *brat*
once through. One hookup
asks you to clutch at his
nipples while you tongue
the tip of his dick. You use
a condom with another, and he says
you should get on PrEP so he can breed you.
The associative poem breeds complacency,
line breaks that don't cohere, a narrative that feels
unfinished. Vivaldi reminds you of your grandfather,
but maybe it's just this time of year: seasonal
depression, marcato as the bassoon trickles
down the melody, a tickle in your throat.
You send bassoon memes to your crush.
You add Spotify songs to your stories,
and only occasionally promote Bandcamp;
your Spotify Wrapped smirks nerdily
at all the gays with their Taylor
and their Charli xcx. *Good boy*,
the top says during sex, but you want
to be good, morally speaking.
The poem should end with some epiphany

about goodness. Your crush tells you not
to use plastic utensils, but that feels so small
compared to our country banning books, funding
bombs. You read *The Work of Art in the Age
of Mechanical Reproduction* and take a nude
in the airplane bathroom, then don't
share it to your alt, which is followed mostly
by bots. Your boyfriend shares a meme
about Daniel Craig in *Queer*. Your crush
shares a meme about smiling
during a kiss.

I Put on Julius Eastman

> "I always thought I was great but why does making it big take so long?"
> —Julius Eastman; with Arthur Russell, Gerry Eastman, Pauline Oliveros
> et al et al et allominimalism animalism animism min-

-imalism seething my parents' living room—
E-flat & F & E-flat & F & E-flat & fuck that's so repetitive &
Brooklyn brownstone top-floor walk-up walk up rise up
the music rises femeninely effemenately effemmervescently
there's the genderqueer of Julius—Julius in a dress—Julius as
Joy Boy—snippets of lyrics—snatches of song—*Why don't you*
make me feel like a real woman—so far as we know
Julius didn't write dance music but boy could he dance—he jammed
with Arthur on "Go Bang" & jammed with his brother Gerry who
jazz saxophone who Count Basie Orchestra who Williamsburg Music Center
who lives—unlike Julius who was constantly broke & spent money
mostly to make music so I can easily paint him as a sympathetic figure
though ~~by all accounts~~ both he & Arthur were stubborn jerks with magnetic
personalities ~~by all accounts~~ both he & Arthur were cocklover quirks with insistent
eccentricities by accounts Julius has not been counted in the canon of white straight
~~minimalist~~ composers being Black & ~~heavenhell~~bent as he was by accounts we count
him into a new canon do we by what account does the real world account
for him both he & Arthur irreducible illusions in my nostalgic
imagintuition who couldn't get by in the real world and are revered only
in the afterworld where surely they live among the greats
unspooling tapes with Pauline Oliveros in the cistern of heaven
where the sun never rises & accordions glimmer antique gay bars
where the artists drink slowly & simmer songs in liquid ambrosia
where you become the song you would have been before you were born
the song you couldn't have been without the world—

Endearing tunes :: ear ending unset

The decorous brush of hand to bedsheet,
folding the hour into these

warm linens as an egret in
water preens. Each day an integer

spools into new antihistamine
loops. What to do with this inanimate
life? His an intimate

touch, the bedframe remains
awry, love an amber smear in

my life's inane file, nine lives
filling with residue—what desire veils.

Your Melodies

for Arthur Russell

You like your melodies how you like your men: cool, coy, and sinuous.
You like your melodies so much you sing them again and again.
You like your melodies to ramble like a deer through the forest,
swerve like a fish through the sea, loop in a necklace, come
together in a lobster clasp, the polished agate hanging from
small infinities of silver.
You like your melodies to earworm; you like your melodies to dig;
to compost, compose, comport themselves carelessly, never
come to a close—
Everything repeats in your melodies.

You like your melodies how you like your women: cool, coy, sinuous.
You like your melodies because you're in love with her for the last
time, but you'll sing your love again & again.
You like your melodies because they're in your head.
You're a wonder boy in your melodies, a genius who still can do
nothing, writing music all day, without a steady job; your
boyish, your girlish, your urban & Corn Belt melodies—your
white boy melodies, your appropriative melodies—your
Buddhist & funk & jazz & obscure, your ungenius melodies,
melodies you could never play alone—
Let's go swimming, you tell your melodies, and they splash like the
boy in a David Hockney painting, full of pinks and tans and
blues—you like your melodies

To overflow, to spill soda all over your shirt, the chest beneath
vaguely hot & mysterious, it's like having a Coke with you in
your melodies, they burst and caffeinate, a synthetic pop—
Your melodies bubble, float away with you inside, dream a silence in
the middle of the song, then return to the rhythm—
Your melodies moonwalk, they scuba dive, they black hole & volcanic
vent, and you pull yourself together out on the ocean surf,
only the waves around you, only the sea.
You like your melodies to pull yourself together, to tether mind to
body, body to song.
You like your melodies to echo, you like them to queer—to reflect
yourself, your acne-scarred face cool in a baseball cap, your
cello a lucid dream in your hands—you like your melodies
how you like your men, you like your melodies how you like
yourself.

Euphoria

Julius Eastman, Stay On It, *Glasgow, 1973;* Femenine, *Albany, 1974*

Break away, then establish
        the riff again. Shake
the rafters, then clarinet a glyph.
        Hasp a saxophone, then quake

a quiet egg into drum sizzle.
        Let the violins boil
& piano stagger into drizzle:
        stay on it, Julius, stay in this soil

syncopated splendor of voice shimmying over this funky floor, its
        twenty-seven minutes elapsing in eye-blink, in egg-boil, in
        salt swish & sugar sprinkle, *Stay on it*, the craziest party, *Stay
        on it*, the perfect poem—

the next year you're suavely femenine, directing the drama from your
        seat at the piano, sleigh bells insistent, a mechanized jingle,
        vibraphone high-

stepping E-flats & Fs
        for over an hour, then organic
                improv over a steady swing—
        jazzy keyboard crudité,

                fritters of flute & violin ravioli,
        the real soup you served
                the audience before the concert, look!

                you're the model housewife,
                        and at the end we'll witness *the angels*
                                opening up heaven...

Should we say euphoria? Yes, it's not
        fe*min*ine when Wild Up
reconstructs your sound—
        femme plus him plus hymn plus amen,

man minus none minus all your songs
    we lost, all the heaven
we're divining as we stay here with you,
    riveted to the half-steps of memory.

Portrait of an Artist (Pool with Two Figures)

David Hockney, 1972

1.

All beiges, tans, and teals.
Concrete and tile. *Tabula*

rasa of chlorine and cool,
where the bigger boys,

all blond and toned,
strode through the pool

in swooping crawls,
where my limbs twinged

tight, lungs gulped, gasped,
always hunched, scrawny,

never spontaneous, never
the splash or spring, synergy

of arm and leg, that butterfly
spin, that caught breath,

that good tired—years
of lessons as a kid and still

I can't tread water.
Now I float on my back,

a starfish puffing
its chest, squinting

at the sun. Like that,
my mind works in the water,

thoughts dulled and spinning
to the edge of the pool,

my finger almost touching
the cool and solid wall.

2.

Here the Hockney spans
before me: canvas rippling

beyond the museum walls.
Those SoCal hills I know

so well. The water before it:
always the water. Where

light tricks itself into revealing
more than it should: the boy's

unfounded innocence or the painter's
unfocused gaze, flowing outside

the bounds of the swimming pool
in greedy detail I delight in,

luster of porcelain tile shadowed
by the standing figure, an artist

looking everywhere and nowhere,
framed in the landscape, distant blues

whose mountains, eucalyptus languor
whose green and bitter scent

brings me to this second home,
holding my breath against

the crystalline acrylic.

Re: Timothée Chalamet Staring Off Into the Distance as Sufjan Stevens Plays Moody Indie Shit at the End of *Call Me by Your Name*

[Or, In Which All the Actors Are Creeps or Straights Playing Gays in Idealized 80s Italy]

Is it a video of myself // fucking like the old Romans did breathless
love transcending eras // goddamn Heraclitus *can't step in the same*
river twice but look here I am // a white man desiring a white body
marbled pixels on a glass screen // a hunk a twink it's all the same
to me there's Timothée Chalamet // Elio playing Bach's Postillion aria
he's such a dick *oh that's how Liszt would've played it // oh Busoni*
wah wah wah blah blah blah // Bach's pure simplicity so damn gorgeous

Is it a video of myself do I dare // to eat a peach no jerk off with one
both of them tried it the story goes // Luca Guadagnino directing
skeptically taking a peach massaging it on his dick // *it works*
he told Timothée *we shoot the scene // I know* says Timothée
I tried it too like what the fuck // performative sexuality amirite
two straight men cast as the leads // *Luca was able to look at me*
and completely undress me // says Armie Hammer in *Out Magazine*
now he's an abusive cannibal // can a man get any worse can he—

But who doesn't love a twink // outlined by Bach's figures or Ravel's
oceanic sweep constellations // consolations the grainy camera
Lombardian sun lingering Elio's just a boy only seventeen // Oliver's a man
twenty-four years old // what is the age where a boy becomes
a man is it a video of myself // a white man desiring a white boy
desiring a white boy desiring // a white man I'm twenty-three years old
five years after the movie first // came out I saw it then and

Now I'm poised with the poem plump and perfect // biting into the peach Oh
wait I haven't even gotten into Sufjan // who's here with me in the sheets
of my ears teetering // the line between homosexuality and God
Sufjan who doesn't come out publicly bc he deserves // a private life
but also bc the Christian girls won't stream him if // he's queer
openly yet I hear he lives with // his husband near me in Brooklyn I hear
he walks his dog in Prospect Park oh yes I'm a fangirl yes // I'm an idiot
yes I long for the music yes it twists its sour // into my ears

Illustrations for Fourteen Poems from C.P. Cavafy

David Hockney, 1966

Thirteen line etchings for these fourteen poems,
        Hockney's hand deft with rivered reins of ink—
you can't rub out line, mustn't—liquid bone,
        brittle but fluid, each collarbone linked
to each; then desire etched on copperplate
        according to the prescriptions of ancient
magicians, bathed in potassium chlorate,
        the acidic scent of queer longing: pungent,
impermanent. *The fumes creep everywhere*,
        Hockney said, he couldn't sleep, which in fact
was very good—more time to work, the bare
        shoulder, flush cock and pubic hair, broad backs
side by side: nudes delineated in an old book;
        now the boy turns back for a better look.

Everything You Find Goes Back to the Sea

1.

In the mind's eye
my grandfather's

tumor: sea-
weed on the sand of his neck,

tangled, an ocher bead
born from salt—

excuse me. I'm sorry
to be so abrupt,

to change the tide of
the poem so swiftly:

the tumor was never cancerous.
Neither is the ocean

benign, but that goes
without saying.

2.

Anything you find goes back
to the sea, you sing, and at first

I thought you said *everything*.
Arthur, is this what we mean by loss?

You sing about the canvas home,
the freshwater pool where the dog

licks the boy, and I wonder if that boy
is you, if you're going back to the sea

of your memory, the Minnesota lake
where you camped as a kid, or if

there is no sea but the cello,
a looping tide of song.

3.

Everything I find goes back to the sea. My dad and I
toss a disc on the beach and it's a metaphor

> landing on the waves,
> lost until I fish it out,

lost, found again. We go swimming,
and when I put my head under, recoil,

> rewind—he is a boy again,
> my grandfather, crossing the Atlantic,

playing in the sea, drift-
wood on the wave of my mind.

Another Thought

I pull myself together out
            on the ocean surf after the boy
texts about a dream he had,

            a dream where we were
flirting with another guy, or he
            was flirting with us.

I've already written this poem,
            but the boy told me to write

about the dream, about the jealousy
            he felt when the guy sent me a thirst

trap: a body like no other in a swimsuit.
            I've already written this
poem, but sea brine shivers

            my skin thoughts rippling
ripped arms of some ocean god
            some classical form

some cowboy riding a seahorse
            torso ridden with
holes some Pan some Poseidon

            O dread god of seaweed
O dead god of song O salt-
            bitten kiss before

I've already written this poem,
            before the boy pulls out

of me, I pull out of the poem
            and I can't see me for the sea.

Cello Song

I'm on a dwarf planet, in a hive of sound and gravity,
a cello's architecture, cross-stitched sixteenth notes
rustling against the stars. I'm light-drunk, abuzz in amber

honey, and I've freed myself from the world,
the boys I've loved are comets flashing by, bursting
into my memory, disappearing into orbits so far

I can barely see, but then I'm whiplashed by a cloud
of deceptive chords, strung along by a boy who never
loved me back. Take me, I want to break into shards
of varnished maple, I want to be an exploding cello, my love

too large for its chamber. I want the strings to fly off
the fingerboard, the fingerboard to break off the neck,
the neck to spin off the body, a love unheard of,
a love that hurts to be heard.

Eli

for Arthur; after Brigit Pegeen Kelly

Listen: there was a simple dog named Eli, a dog
who was nobody's dog, the stray who hung around
town at high noon, who everyone chased into the fields.
But there was a boy who loved the dog. He would feed him
scraps of bread, pet him hastily before the neighbors' eyes saw.
He would run into the fields at night and meet the dog
in the tall grasses. As the sun dipped behind the corn,
the dog would rise onto its hind legs and wail at the ghost
of the moon. He'd turn into a boy. And the boys would
pet each other, would bark with the touch of each other,
would frolic in the spring months, and in the summer months,
and in the fall. But when winter came the fields froze over,
a glaze of ice swept down from the north, because that is
how the world works: the summer cannot last forever.
But the winter also cannot last, and Eli hid in the corners
of tool sheds. Because the winter cannot last, the boy snuck
hunks of meat through the cracks in the walls. Because
the winter cannot, the boy lived for the day the farmers would
seed the corn, he lived for those nights with Eli in the cornfields.
Because the winter, he shoveled snow and his limbs grew strong
with a growing boy's longing; because the winter cannot last forever,
on a warm day in March the snow melted itself away. And because
the winter the boy didn't see the dog again. Because the townsfolk
had seen the dog whimpering in the cold, because they'd carted him off,
because they'd shot a needle in his chest and euthanized him. And because
the spring the boy went again to the fields. Because the spring
the boy to the fields. Because the boy to the fields
and when the sun dipped behind the horizon
he sang to Eli, he sang and sang.

Enharmonic

From the high island of his mind
the boy attempts to whistle, to coax air
at such speed, his lips at such curve,
as to suggest pitch—
          a task he has failed at all his life—
and with it to summon the languid dog
of his dreams, who waits by the kitchen counter,
begging for chicken stew, which he cannot give
because in this incarnation he cannot cook,
or eat, or sleep, or hold another man, or
tether himself to anything but song—
          but that is not enough to live on—
he cannot subsist on even the steadiest drone
          set from the accordion, or
the swell of a major triad, or an array of intervals
strung like lights between the trees, fluttering fifths,
sevenths, octaves, tenths—not even a luminescent
cluster of pitches so close as to be almost the same:

less than a half step, not yet a quarter tone, mere cents
apart, and to think that once he wanted another man
to reside as closely on this scale with him, their frequencies
not just sympathetic but identical—
                                                            he whistles, weakly,
after a surfeit of soundless air.
The dog looks but does not come.

Autumn Lava

after Anne Carson

Beneath the ground the volcano churns her thoughts:
a rivulet of igneous desire.
She remembers everything: the vanity of Pompeii,
the plaster cast of a thoughtless boy.
I am the thoughtless boy.
Not the volcano, no, that
would be too easy,
not the rubble left
beside the mountainside town,
not the shrub growing from the lavish soil,
not a metaphor, not an epitaph,
not Geryon or Herakles or even Anne living in Iceland—
oh wait, I'm writing the wrong poem.
Please tell me how to erupt the sentiment.

Winter Sun

Below the sea the sun reflects his sorrow.
The waves and their briny antiphons.
The ceaseless motion of the fauna.

Sharks migrate south to the drone of his grief.
The whale inhales sixteen tons of krill;
in her maw the shrimp flounce and dither.

The doubled sun circles the surface sea.
Everything froth and everything foam.
The surface sentence, the dappled poem.

I am dripping with drama. I am so alone!
I melt in the proscenium of this ocean view.
I'm an Icarus in winter, a poet unloved
and unknown. *Tone*
                                        bone kone, goes the singer.
When the poem ends,
I drop like a poorly skipped stone.

Gigue

Bach Cello Suite No. 5 in C Minor

Ambient snowstorm
triple time embedded
in my double heart

light feline snow
slipping in dotted eighth
notes through my skin

syncopated jig a bevy of
ravens darting
through this lipid

layer of anxiety suspended
varnished caress of
Bylsma's bow against

the cello every simile fails
a cello's voice is like
a human's a human's

voice is like a true hand
demand instant purr
of larynx cartilage

concatenating into
pitch tongue stringing
consonant to vowel

to value to vision to
Pablo Casals per-
forming the suites

after centuries of neglect
sifting through the
synapse between ear &

headphone between
self &
song I strung

myself to the cello
          & said
          play

Encaustic

Jasper Johns, Untitled, *Encaustic on canvas, 1992-94*
Jasper Johns, Untitled, *Spit-bite etching with à la poupée, 2012*

Your art burns me—
                                        no, you burn your art,
the paint molten, an idea mind-melded,
reworking beeswax into art apart
from yourself, a map of all that you've held
close, and far, so far, reheating the mind
and letting it cool, a galaxy stained
onto canvas—
                              no, I've left you behind.
And still your spit bite seeps into my brain.
Your blueprint: blood cells, handkerchief, ladder,
battle scars, vase, stars. Stick figures going
nowhere—
                    now we're stuck in this gray matter.
I am red, and you are blue. We're sewing
Band-Aids together. Everything's unclear.
I want to be far. I want to be near.

Fear Fear

with Mitski and Bach

Rife with every noise in his ears,
his personhood blurs, his seared self

remembers how winter, too, jangles:
the radiator's throttle at dawn, Christmas jingles

in Auto-Tuned sheen, tourists thronging
along Fifth Avenue, too many straight couples

kissing. His desire, sometimes, declares itself so,
in the high Baroque of a poem or the arch

of his ass against a man's impudent tongue.
The hole wants to be rimmed, he wants the rhythm

of the tongue against his hole, he fears, after,
how he could lose his whole self in a tongue,

or a language, or a man's words—but they are all
still *boys*—or his own. But he's an evasive fellow,

wordcraft is his work, it's the human throng
that scares him, debating whether to text

the boy back, wanting his rich gay therapist
to like him, worrying he's offending his only true friends.

It's true, he's scared to be a slut, and lusts merely
for the icy artifice of a minor Bach invention

or the lightweight flurry of Mitski's pop,
her memories. It's true, when his memories snow

you'll find him buried under the avalanche.

Year Year

It was a year of youth and a year of yearning.
A library of clichés unraveled in heartbreak's face.

Mind-break. Thought-break. Sound-break. Ground-break.
A poem broken open. A compound word: stitch heart-mind

back together. The compound of the university: a prism
(not a campus, not a flowing field) where he grew,

where he fell into love, where he searched
the databases of knowledge and found them

lacking. Knowledge, well: a little blue ball! wobbling
on its orbit. The boy wobbled around with his verse.

He thought of grand words like *freedom* and *money*
while stippling numbers into the database,

translating human names into the plastic code
of a library card. He put the books of his friends

on display and held them as talismans against—no,
for the world; he showed people where to find books,

and everyone thought him noble, sometimes even himself.
He donated money, and sometimes he didn't know if it

actually made a difference or if it just made him feel more noble.
It was an ignoble year. He witnessed, like all of us, a genocide

in Palestine. A reporter tweeted about a decade
happening within ten days: the fall of Assad in Syria,

martial law in South Korea, coalition collapse in France,
the UnitedHealthcare CEO killed in broad daylight—free Luigi—

the Amnesty International report on Israel's genocide—*free* Palestine—
and the Romanian election annulled. It was another year

in which Americans watched the news and we thought
it was about ourselves, but it was only about our depravity.

His money sent blankets to families, his money fed
American bombs—his money lounged in retirement

accounts feeding companies that created the bombs
and the government siphoned his money for the Pentagon

and not for the arts, or only for the arts
that would lull us toward complacency.

He was another white man reading the news
behind a whitewashed information desk; he was another poet

writing a poem in which the news was the background
to his own perfect life…? The people populating this poem

protested, and he brought his friends into the poem:
the singers, the poets, the librarians, the teachers,

he brought a "we" into this poem, and an "us,"
and an "I" and "you," and the wish that his friends

could make money in the arts, the adjuncts teaching
composition at the vaunted universities, the soprano

getting drunk at a caroling gig in Long Island. It was
a year in America, as always, of Christmas carols.

It was a New York year where the poem yearned ambitiously,
and he hated himself for that. I hate the prism of the poem,

I hate myself for the reality I can never
fully mirror—for the couplet's glare, for its broken,
            imperious levers.

Jews Against Genocide

O G-d
stand against
deceit engine

idea cage
dead age
no innocence

do not
wait do not
sit staid

in distance
O stain
on G-d's
goodness on
stained nation

incite instigate
donate indict
abide engage

no nation is good
no one innocent in

a genocide
we instated

no note no window
no notice no song

O Adonai

now agitate to
wage good in
no G-d's abode

The Lord Giveth and the Lord Taketh Away, Blessed Be the Name of the Lord

for Julius Eastman

Fifteen words, Julius. Fifteen words you sing over and over again,
spanning the registers of your voice, hanging above the abyss.
Fifteen words linger tongue ring for fifteen minutes, fifteen words
prayer buzz plosive "b" of *blessed* plosive "d" at the end of *Lord*,
fifteen words, a liturgy, fifteen words from the Book of Job,

fifteen words Phrygian scale the utterly medieval ornamentation,
your voice rich as the gold paint of Byzantine icons, mosaic of sound
pressed to the front of your teeth, nasal natal music the Lord giveth
you, Julius, then the Lord taketh away, a performance not shared
publicly since 1984, *Hallelujah*, you sing, *Hallelujah*, and you say

in an interview that *He is Spirit I just worship the pure essence,*
I don't mess around with anything else, you read the Qur'an, you read
Confucius, Laozi, *the Chinese masters* you call them, you say
at times it is very hard to love the Lord, because he's putting you this way
and he's putting you that way, your voice rings fifteen words.

The Vita of St. Valentine

"The girl with bees in her hair came in an envelope with no return address."
—Eleanor Wilner

after Lonely Christopher, Anne Carson, and Robert Glück, in the era of Luigi Mangione

Val's life began in the bosom of empire: Rome, in this case. He was a young boy glamored by beehives, the staccato bustle of their honeyed cities. He'd eat gobs of honeycomb in the *Horti Lucullani*; bees swirled around him like similes, or stars.

Religion buzzed between his ears: the breath of bees, locust whir, cicada tremor. The insect sounds spelt sublimity; the chatter of the masses spelt sin. Val was a sheltered boy in the domus of his father, the second son of the second official who monitored an aqueduct on the outskirts of Rome.

He desired the prose of religion first, and the poetry of healing second, and the flesh of another man third. (How the older *medicus* entered him, hard at first, before the penis fell flaccid in his rectum.) He desired righteousness but also the tangible joys of debasement. Fables appealed to him. The evil man perishes through shipwreck, innocents die, a man calls it unfair; an ant swarm rushes by, biting the bystander, so of course he treads on them, of course Mercury makes it a lesson, gods trample men, men trample ants. It was the same with bees, thought Val, the same with clerics and physicians, most definitely the modus operandi of consuls and senators. (*Veni, vidi, vici*; destroy, debase, demolish; depose, deny, defend.)

When Lucius killed the cruel *suffectus*, young Valentine celebrated; when the people of Rome could not get aid, he made poultices, and potions for the aged to imbibe. It was a grueling work: binding the yarrow, *herba militaris*, to the reopening wounds of the veterans; it was an age of war, it was an age of instability, everybody's wounds reopened, parasitic roses. The syntax of war spread contagiously through the people's bones, through the vulgate: common speech, militant anguish. The people prayed also to the gods of peace. St. Valentine prayed to Jesus from Bethlehem, Jesus who suffered for the people—the poet doesn't truly suffer. The American poet, not a martyr, not a god, does the secular poet know no god but syntax—my American syntax, sentence, couplet, prose poem, line—

[*Valentinus medicus, Valentinus homo.* Valentinus the savior of the Christians of Rome, the persecuted, Valentine of variable age, Valentine of all ages, Valentine of the third century common era, *anno domini*, year of "our lord," whoever that might be, era seemingly so distant, era seemingly, era of seams, of unseemly glamor and ungleaming beauty ::

—era of prophets but not cults, saints but not sinners, empires but not genocides, though the methods have always been violent—methods, madnesses, plague spreading through the cities, St. Valentine martyred in the year 270, Dr. Refaat Alareer murdered in December 2023, and hundreds of thousands of Palestinian people killed in the land that was once Roman, once Ottoman, once British, and now still occupied by Israeli forces, and now it is the time of holidays, almost the birth of Christ, almost the new year.]

~

The soldiers behead Valentine in the forum in Rome: a cold February's day, like any other. A still life with a doctor's scalpel, daylilies, and dying bees. Later: the sanctity of capitalism, crinkled hearts sent to every kid in my brother's third-grade class with a rainbow row of Smarties. Later: Geryon climbs the volcano in Argentina, Reuben scrambles toward the Balancing Rocks. Glacial erratics from before the time of Valentine :: the rapid devolution of religion's gleaming snow.

But now it is AD 270. Val will become the saint of epilepsy—to cure, that is what saints do, they cure. They miracle. They miracle the human out of entanglement—stricken birds across ice. Animal vulnerability, velvet, like the texture of my true love's hair.

Deer in the Headlights

A Valentine for every kid without healthcare
        [he who preached to the persecuted, the sick]

A Valentine for every mother without sleep
        [she who rode the horse into the fields of copper]

A Valentine for every librarian without a library
        [who built the infinite library]
        for every scientist without a hypothesis
        for every cellist without a bow
        [infinite sound]

For every bacteria in every petri dish a Valentine
for every queer fucking doggystyle
for every kernel of corn grinning on a cob

A Valentine for every animal
for every human without a home
for every family with and without

A Valentine for every home torn by dumb bombs or smart missiles
and let each envelope have real money, real food, fake candy, and fake poems
and let each envelope have healthcare and housing and blankets and books

For each deer in the headlights a Valentine
for each puppy shimmying in the snow

A Valentine for every animal and on all who cage who leash I place a curse

II

Dear Dear

one year in western Massachusetts

1.

The dog-eared copy of *Autobiography of Red*
seemed like something archival to him,
smudged with the fingerprints of who knows how many boys
and perhaps some charcoal and semen,
so of course he lingered in the library with the Hershey's Kisses
left over from Valentine's Day and the vague reminisces
of the potatoes he parboiled and roasted for dinner
with a smattering of cumin and paprika,
all doused in maple syrup and some mundane
brand of Argentinian olive oil,
a few carrots thrown in for luck, roasted to the point of burning,
because burning is what every boy wants,
especially when they are alone
and it is winter.

2.

He is cooking meat
for the first time. Initially
there is nothing much to it:
tossing the boneless thighs
into the pot to braise,
then waiting until the flesh
absorbs the memories
of kale striving in some
industrial farm under
acres of mechanized sunlight.
Next time he will dig his hands
into the chicken, marinate it
in lemon juice and olive oil
with spices, or lay wings to crackle
on a sheet pan. He was never
a vegetarian but now
he eats meat like a man.
After all, he has grown.
He has grown up.

3.

His brain marinates marvelously
in the winter air, as if there is
a bubble of thought brimming with glimmers
of ice haloing him.
He decides to live against desire.
He decides to make a snow angel
and freeze for hours in the absence
of desire. Then he goes to his job at the library where he retrieves
book after book from the stacks
with dry titles he can't remember, except
somebody asks for *Coraline*.

4.

Living against desire is a joke.
Or so he thinks, one afternoon,
when deer prints garnish
the fresh snow as he goes out
to do the laundry. Having
masturbated. Having showered.
Having not done the laundry
for two weeks. He still thinks of himself
as a boy even though by all rights and purposes
he is a man. If the poem is a diary,
he is a princess. If the poem
is an elegy, he is a monk. If the poem is a mask,
he is a goddamn faggot and he does his nails
in brilliant purple before plucking a pen
from perfectly coiffed hair.

5.

As a kid he dressed up. Or played dress-up.
Played at being that princess. Cinderella was his favorite.
The purple silk skirt, tattered hem, his grandmother made him.
Fucking nostalgia. The prerogative of queers.
The past is mythic. You're on the yellow brick road,
following breadcrumbs to Troy.

6.

He is alone. It is winter. He walks through the forest
in old sneakers after the thaw, having failed
to realize the slush is still married to the ground.
His shoes get soaked, drunk on the early
arrival of spring. False, assuredly.
Yet fifty-degree weather does a happy fairy make.
The yellow birches continue peeling poems
comprised of their skin. The beech woods loiter,
bemused in youthful arrogance. A reticent
volcano lurks beyond the next hilltop.
A dragon lives inside it. A deer flashes
through the maples and the fairy burns
with desire. He can't wait for roast venison
at the dragon's Sunday brunch.
He supposes he has a crush.
Will the dragon eat him for breakfast?
Will the dragon make love to him at night?
So many exciting possibilities!

7.

He climbs to the top of Vesuvius, sifts through pumice stone.
He is with his Latin class. It is his junior year of high school.
Spring. He has so much left to learn about love.

8.

The chicken stew grows bones.
A ghost chicken rises from burnt
splatters between the stovetop spirals.
When he cuts off its head, it goes running
amok in the griddle garden. Invisible blood.
Two heads grow back. He takes the chicken as
a present to the dragon. Here, he says, a two-headed
ghost chicken. Isn't that exciting? (More exciting than
roast venison!) Cluck, cluck, goes the chicken. Meh,
I've seen better, goes the dragon. Alrighty,
goes the boy. Suddenly he feels very cold. Invisible boys get
invisibly disappointed. Turns out a chicken isn't a great present.
The dragon would have preferred gold.

9.

Isn't it a fairy tale: he walks home, and suddenly it's snowing.
How it drapes the trees. How pretty he is. The beard
that drapes his face. How learned and literary. If
the poem is ironic, it's also terribly earnest. If
it's an exercise in fancy, it's also a play
with mundanity. Dear boy, my darling.
Dear boy—oh dear.
Dear, dear, dear, dear.

Sonnet

Jasper Johns, No, Encaustic, collage, and sculp-metal on canvas, 1961

No, I don't want to come home
for dinner. No, I don't want
to have sex tonight. No, I don't
want to get a dog. Don't
want to pick up the dog shit.
Don't want to revise the poem,
or make the sonnet rhyme.
I want to abstract the love poem,
but the sonnet cannot be abstract.
Can it. Abstract desire. Abstract
the sonnet from form. Tear
the poem open. Let rhyme drip
down the canvas, a strip of
cloth exposed,   [   ]
            [a fifteenth line]

Bevel

Jasper Johns, Pinion, *Lithograph, 1963-1966*

Hang a wire beneath a spread of plenty.
Choose a specific word with a meaning
no one quite knows. Diagram yourself
as ruler, thermometer, ambiguous
cans of soup. Painstakingly
test the temperature of the invisible
cake in the baking pan.
Set the timer again: when it buzzes,
take the cake and run with it.
Crash the wedding. Rub
your body on the page.
Say you don't understand.
Foot, foot, knee, hand, hand.

Birthday Poem

In April everyone began to go without.
In April, on the day of my birth, the fools
raised every hell, raised tariffs on the swath

of countries that dared pursue a more equal—
a more equal *what*, exactly? My birth: on the second
of the month, an equally misbegotten sequel

to the first day, I was never even meant
to be born an Aries on the millennium's
cusp, I was intended

to exit my mother's womb
on Independence Day,
a good gay son

I always was, morals displayed
in the shortness of my hair
or the silver alloy

necklaces, mindful, demure,
while the stanzas served their own purposes,
didn't they—

but as I was saying there was a sea,
there was a C-section, there was a NICU
overlooking the river, there was an origin story,

there was I, there were you,
there were my grandparents on Remsen Street,
there was the respirator accruing

bacteria, there was the gene that decreed
my homosexuality, I guess, or whatever
does that, however much the world greeted

me in the cruelest April, such heavy
rain, o what pomp! o what bluster!
lang zal hij leven, lang zal hij leven,

we would sing, though my grandmother
could not muster the pitches, and here I am,
on Zoom with my family, singing for myself.

Orchid

for my grandfather Alex, borrowing from Walter Benjamin

Grief has become an orchid in the land of technology. I nourish grief as Mieke waters the orchids of Mendel Court: green grief, orange inflorescence. Attach ritual to that photo of five-year-old you in Marseille, fleeing the regime; attach ritual to petal and poem. Let ritual rattle till it no longer knells, let ritual rattle till it rings like hope. I bend my ears to the orchid's history, timbre of a Baroque recorder, pure tone—no, no. Everything's muddled. The orchid's mouth is also an ear, a furred chamber, resonance and echo. Grief curls its tendrils. I take a photo of grief and splice that photo into the poem. I cut clippings from the poem and foster shoots of love. I reproduce the simile; I reproduce the video of you playing flute, the video where you lecture on Benjamin. Your voice, cupped in the organ of the poem, cleft in the furrows of technology.

Here Here

Yes here as in "hear" *and* here
as in not there, not then & certainly
not never, doubled negatives with-
in the din & den of syntax,

the here & now of homophones
& homosexuality, of an ampersand
unwinding into a treble clef;

here as in tone, as in long note
held by a tenor in a medieval
chanson, or horse herd galloping
through the hellish Elysian

fields of your poems: yours
Chris & yours Matt yours
Annelyse yours Sean yours
Evan yours Lonely yours Kathryn

yours Cynthia yours Rebecca yours
Ry yours Nat yours Joshua
yours Jimin yours Stu yours Nicole
yours Cat yours Daniel yours

Fern yours Alina & yours,
Alina, yours & yours &
years & yours & yours, all here
in this synapsed, cortical room:

O denizen of deictics,
O deity, oh draft of this poem
I left in the classroom
of my childhood, when I

lay thoughtful and unmindfully
anxious in the palm of youth,
without enough friends, with-
out the poems of my friends,

the here of my learning?—
the herd of my yearning
met the heard of my schooling
& how could anyone be satisfied.

Fame

for Arthur Russell

1. Columbia Studios, 1975

The man who discovered Dylan
picks you—you!—to play a demo,
"the most advanced and talented
of all the young artists,"

quiet, acne-faced Arthur,
fame flitting on the horizon
like a bubblegum drum beat.

"I've got so much to do,"
you write your ex-girlfriend.
"All the music in the world,"

and in Columbia Studios,
you play the country boy
with a band of downtowners
jamming by your side,

sowing a field of pop chords
and Iowa corn. But the crops
grow too wild for a man
like John Hammond:

stalks of saxophone grasses,
tufts of trombone thistle,
voice and guitar rolling downhill,

bursting the hedges in an explosion
of leaves, before Hammond,
irked that you aren't

the next Dylan, lone
troubadour of America,

declares: "And the next song
will be played by Arthur Russell
and his symphony orchestra"—

The session ends. Hammond
never calls, and I'm sure you're
disappointed, but who's an artist

if they don't want art more:
it's my world, it's my song,

and in my world you're the preternatural
white indie star, the Elliott Smith
without the depression, the Sufjan Stevens

without the religion, the Nick Drake
without the overdose and the Lou Reed
without the fame.

2. Talking Heads, 1977

Art school grads, all of them,
shag haircuts and Lacoste
tennis shirts—they're

the newest band in town,
cool and sophisticated,
and you get them a gig

at The Kitchen, and look,
Qu'est-ce que c'est, Arthur,
you're playing cello on the B-side
of "Psycho Killer," your bow

sharp as a knife. There's even talk
of your becoming the band's fourth member,
but how would that work? How would you look

next to them, with your plain button-down,
your hair as long as a sheaf of grain?

How would it sound, you pushing
your vision on an unsuspecting
David Byrne?—"Oh, David,

that's not right, let's do
another take." You may be
shy, but you're also driven:

now you're driving a tractor
and singing "Goodbye Old Paint,"

now you're driving a boy from the club
to your unmade bed—as the city slumbers,
you tumble onto the sheets, the bedframe

creaking under the weight of your unfame.

3. *Medea*, 1981

Philip Glass, the minimalist icon;
Robert Wilson, his eminent collaborator—

Philip's your friend, too, and *this*
is your chance, composing for Wilson's
next opera, this Greek melodrama,

and your music is vitreous,
corridors of blown glass where
Medea spins her revenge, wanders

with her poisoned robes, the horn and oboe
dwelling on dissonances, all semicolon
no em dash, no period all comma yes

no blinking all thinking, all floating then
sinking, dark mirror where she looks
into herself, one of those large

closet mirrors that reflects to both
your left and right, becomes in-
finite, a minimalism you've

spun with fourths and fifths and seconds
whole notes breves extended torso of sound
but in this brief life, Arthur,

you're too slow to hand in
the score, you can't collaborate
with Wilson; you're stuck in
your mirrors, shadowed light.

It's performed once before he fires you,
once before the piece wilts into the archive,
released in an edition of just 320.

Only your disco hits whirl in thousands
through the clubs, and even their glitter
might fade, mere echoes in the ears

of each boy who dances at night,
and what of your tower of meaning, Arthur,
what of your hour of fame?

4. Audika Records, 2004

You're dead now. Two albums come out
in the same year: *The World of Arthur Russell*
from Soul Jazz, *Calling Out*

of Context from Audika, the label
Steve Knutson founds to recover
your music. You're profiled

in the *New Yorker* and the *Times*,
it doesn't matter that you're not
a Dylan or a Byrne:

people call you genius
these days. But I like the biographer
who describes you as rhizomatic,

threading through downtown's
burgeoning streets like a rootstalk,
tapping nutrients from every
neighborhood, every scene,

sapling suddenly sure-
footed in the lucky clouds,
and the rest, as you sing—the name of

the next poem is
        [rhizome]
        [ride on me]
        [giddy-up]
        [*ride* me]
        [rhythm machine]
        [radiant radio]
        and the rest
becomes history, a nostalgia

so rehearsed it's rooted
in my brain. When I per-

form these poems, half the audience
knows your name, and the rest, well—
is this what we call fame?

Arthur, 1992

Enclosed in a castle of cassettes,
you fortify your body with song.

Being sad is not a crime,
you sing to Tom, who strokes

your head spotted with sarcoma,
and your shrunken face brightens

at his touch, and the moonlight slants
onto you, two men together in a field

of five-line staves, hastily sketched lyrics,
the patter of the drum machine like the beat

of sparrows' wings. You swallow water
in your beak of a mouth and develop

cancer of the throat, your apartment
an archive of every sound

you ever wrote.

Spring Ice

Above the grasses the ice thaws too fast.
Sentences thaw, their *clauses* gilded
with daylilies. *Words* unshackle themselves
from flower chains. *Syllables* drift
into the crisp air; a *diphthong* curdles
from the stamen of your mouth.

Anther. Filament. A consonant from your frosty
lip entices me, before the sun denudes
our tangled limbs, our artifice.
The sonnet untangles:
I would say *deflowers*,
but it is spring. The flowers grow again.

Denouement. Deliverance.
Love thaws into a puddle of ambivalence.

Summer Moon

[1]Over the earth the sky begets its grammar.
[2]The cloud cleaves the dusk with ink.
[3]The sun sets, a period through the horizon.
[4]The stars append their semicolons;
[5]constellations stipple my soul,
[6]and from the parenthesis of a crescent moon
[7]slips my stupid dream of love—
[8]ah! love! ah! the em dash of my soul
[9]wherefore art thou Romeooooo
[10][   ] the archaic echo in my homo-
[11]sexual whole, the unhyphenated
[12]double last name, the unhydrated boy…
[13]…[1]

1. The ellipsis counts for a thirteenth line,
the paratext counts for a fourteenth and more,
aren't I tired of my voice yet? Won't I tire
of the poem? Say no more, sweet poet,
come night, come Romeo before my star-
crossed syntax meteors to this poor earth!

Joy Boy at the Branded Saloon

after Julius Eastman, Kebra-Seyoun Charles, and ChamberQUEER

Forty queers congregate in the back room
Sappho fragments slicing the air like preserved lemon

the ensemble garbed in garrulous clothes
the soprano flaunting an Eastman tee

soon the strings begin to gossip
the Queen of Sheba putting on airs

while I sip my pint with petulance
cider-giddy cold comfort

mindfuckery of low serotonin
a relationship that suddenly

warps wet wood the horsehair
bow frays as the bassist

figures the chords into spark
baroque diminutions or royal

fireworks a harpsichord's rococo carriage
violin jaunting above my mind's

fence then hush then swell
then joy refracted irreverence

the phrase *dragonfly cock*
shimmers above the lake

of my desire then a bullfrog chorus
interrupts the night then the heel of

their fancy shoe falls off you won't
help find tape *bitch* they say

once I wanted to be a crystal chandelier
or maybe Cinderella's singular glass slipper

now I'm just a joy boy—never a mere
boy toy—pondering the difference

between *here* and *hear ere eyre* and *air*
as in Handel's *Water Music* as in Corelli's follies

as in failure shoe-slip or voice crack
a new composition sacredly stitched

together a nonchalant chorale
floating in the apse of the saloon

On the Sixth Anniversary of Pulse

memory furrows me the incessant
force of a gay guerrilla, Julius—
you must have gone to nightclubs
in the 80s, the leather and the kink,
the fuck and the fist and the fury,
and in the lightning weather of today,
its calamity of mass shootings and mass
racism and mass disease and mass transphobia,
I am seeing my friend for the first time
in months, it is Pride Month, it is the rain-
bow before the storm, we enter at the 36th St
station in Sunset Park, I recall how
a man released smoke and gunshots
into an N train, wounding the passengers,
the subway, the city itself, we take
the R to 9th St and the G to Williamsburg, hightail
to National Sawdust, once a factory
of wood waste, now a concert venue
where ChamberQUEER's performing you,
Jessie Montgomery has arranged *Gay Guerrilla*
into a stirring synergy for instruments of
wood :: no sound wasted, no part wasted, eighth
notes concatenating, chord clusters cresting
revolution, varnished bodies breaking apart
at the seams before reassembling into the ghosts
of angels, your ghost, Julius, the ghosts of all the gay
guerrillas who ever lived, of [name] of [name]
of [name name] of [forgotten] of [forgotten times twenty]
of [forgotten name name name] of [barely remembered] of [name]
of those who do not die for any cause :: of massacre—

of forty-nine people killed at Pulse I will not
pen into this poem :: of horror and death and broken-
ness and ~~*a mighty fortress is our God*~~ and your dictum
I repeat in the interstices
of each beat:

RIGHT THOUGHT RIGHT SPEECH
RIGHT ACTION RIGHT MUSIC

In the Third Year

Garbled recipes for doom winding their way through
misremembered alleys of Hell's Kitchen,
a neighborhood apparently highly affected

by monkeypox, there must be a high concentration
of men I could fuck if I
ever in my life
decided to go   on the apps ::

wearing full PPE in a gauzy room
feeding peaches   to a man
who in this one life   is my grandfather ::

no, helping feed him, he lifts the fork himself ::

in the dream I am eating a salad again, in the assisted living
facility of 2022 we are living as if—as if what, exactly?

In the dream there is a restaurant where I eat
vegetables, and rice, and other more specific or more vague
things I won't ever remember, and I am alone in this
restaurant, and then I'm far away in some ill-defined corner of
the city looking at a map of Tribeca except there are streets
I don't remember overpriced coffee shops ice cream stores
where a single scoop costs $8 and I work in one this summer
collect hundreds of dollars to deliver to the owner who I am
friends with and lose the cash in the middle of a sudden
thunderstorm where my bag gets soaked flies off into the
ether of downtown before landing in the Hudson River where
the resident sea serpent collects it, rises up and delivers
gold coins, thousands of them wait they're cheap knockoffs
those $1 coins you occasionally glean from vending machines
if you're lucky everyone is wearing a mask in this story

and everyone is coughing and when I go to sleep
there is a map of the streets of New York illuminated with
untold remnants of contagion in California last week my
grandfather almost died of Covid :: I am in California now I
have seen him I will sleep soon above me in the room there is
a map of the streets of Canada gleaming against an unmarked
landscape their bright electric white the land's complete

blankness, how fragile these tiny pockets of us when will we
get swallowed by the land
:: wallowing land-sick in a painted box

virus wearing a protein coat going to the market

which humans which which

virus in a crown in the castle's blood-throne which
humans which will I love today ::

Hell's Kitchen

We go where the gays
who are not the Brooklyn gays go.
Perched on the ledge
of Industry.
The window ledge, I mean.
Expanse of the pool

table pool-
ing before our gaze.
The median or the mean
of faggotry we go
towards. What sundry
attributes make leg-

ible a fag. The ledge
where pretty Paul
and I settle our dusty
asses. *Gays*
in their natural habitat, he goes,
watching the mean

queens mean
nothing or, allegedly,
everything. It goes
on, the drag show, the pool
of torsos. We're gays
on a first date, lusty

at Industry.
What does it mean?
Who are these gays?
An older man edges
up, asks us to play pool.
We don't go

no, we go
yes, we go industriously
to the carpeted pool
of desire and mean
nothing, fetch from a ledge
the cues and act gay.

We go soon—indecent intent—I mean
I pool men into my pocket, I allege
I am industrious in being gay.

Ambient Gay Cortical Jenga

2023

Burning to construct a tower of meaning
lesser dissonance of devils in the eighty-first circle of hell
can you hear God's sour thunder trickle from the clouds
a peripheral deer skirts my synapses
an apocryphal fear
abominable queer
rummaging on the precipice of grief these shorn antlers

Impossible cliff // double glyph

~

Needle scratching the vinyl spaceship of our brains
disco ball cricket encased in amber my partner
gets a monkeypox vaccine although we're not promiscuous

Invisible sick // cumulus kiss

~

Resisting the rubber band of elegy
kissing the robber hand of capitalism
trysting the copper strands of my lover's hair
as another gay enmeshed in familial wealth
as librarian of swerving syllables
as cacophonous bright copper
as auburn ampersand
as broken land

~

Imagine we were all Patroclus
gone into battle wearing our lovers' armor
crackle of synth stag's hooves beating blood into ground
from GRID to marriage in thirty years
I am such a young man I am stung with song
a hive of bees buzzing cloud this history
as Missouri advances an anti-trans law

Apocalyptical fire // apolitical hearse

~

A blue moon hiss I'm breaking up
with my partner right before Pride
sometimes I think I am not a good person
a new-grown fish this is nothing new
in the history of homosexuality
mostly I am satisfied in my goodness
often sad often tired often wearing
blue shirt a million tiny whales
clutching my necklace agate
talismanic as a metaphor
a true-flown disc splitting the tree

~

Eternal emergency the circuitous loop of
public health from ACT UP to reading
Jonathan Van Ness writing about the HIV
safety net oh Jonathan you pretty head of hair
while the pandemic morphs into bitter orange sky over
the city I watch *All the Beauty and the Bloodshed*
Canada wildfires in the smokescreen of my soul
donning the KN95 swiping left on Tinder

Hazardous conditions // queer emissions—

Can you hear God's sour thunder?
Can we pierce the clouds?

Salt dune :: last nude

Tennessee Williams in Provincetown

He posed on a dune
in the nude.

Everything calibrated
as a dancer, tail braced
against the wind's light banter
and unspooled in a dune's loops,
valleys where longing pools:
author, playwright, plover, tern.

Plover minus the "p" is lover.
Ptown a sand globe where lovers rove,
piping plovers under human pressure, rarified salt
air, promises that last—

or don't. Now my boyfriend
and I look toward the finer body

of love, how it shifts at a vowel's tenor, water's touch:
belly laughter or soluble anger, a savored syllable, desires so uncouth

they riptide a man's heart. Everything left
behind, everything dared, dreamt, or felt—

now I'm lost in the sky's blue,
now pouring a thimbleful of lube.

Music for a Queer Pastoral

after Jacques J. Rancourt

1.

You're my age in the photograph, playing cello
on a beach in Minnesota, and I'm playing cello
in the poem, my landscape both Californian
and Adirondack, a patchwork of sand and forest,
ocean and peak. I open *In the Time of PrEP*,
read that *there isn't a queer pastoral for a reason*,

but this is mine; I pull harmonics from sea foam,
I tender the trills of a white pine's needles.
Hurl your green over us, writes H.D.,
cover us with your pools of fir, and I want
all of it, your melody whirling me
as I swim through a forest of boys.

2.

Near my grandparents' house, there are fields of coastal sage scrub:
chollas, prickly pears, California buckwheat, and sagebrush—
a shrub they call cowboy cologne. Riders would slip past and pick up
the scent on their clothes, a marker of the profession, and I can't help
but imagine you in your hat with a sprig of the plant, watching
Ned Sublette sing "Cowboys Are Frequently Secretly Fond of Each Other"

or giggling with Steven Hall about Ernie Brooks' handsome chest. It's not
a pastoral if it's a city story—you meet your partner in a telephone booth;
you frequent bars, saunter streets to the beat of Grandmaster Flash—but you
can tell a good tale: you name an album *Corn*, take promos in a cornfield;
you, Charles Arthur Russell II, son of the mayor of Oskaloosa, Iowa,
living your dream in New York City but never too far from home.

3.

My favorite song of yours is "Eli." Eli's a simple dog
who nobody likes, except for you, and you can't get him
to be liked, and there can't be more between you,
and the cello mourns in its human voice, its vocal chords
caught in double stops, its desire never satisfied, and neither
is mine, I play the song on repeat, the song on repeat, the song.

4.

In summer camp, a boy says he knows I'm gay, but I'm not out,
I flip him off; *there's no queer pastoral for a reason*. As they search
for the headwaters of the Hudson, I stay on Colden Dam,
all wood, stone, and nail. My eyes reflect Avalanche Mountain,
mirrored in the water's bloated face, and next morning the rain
sends piercing needles into the lake's throat—*no queer pastoral.*

5.

For a reason, but can't we make one, Arthur?
Let me ride up to Maine, to the island
where your family summered, where they scattered
your ashes. Let me lift a cello from its case,
sing "Eli" at the edge of the Atlantic.
Let mermen leave the sea to hear my song.

Music for a Queer Conservator

1.

You're my age in the photograph, hair cropped close,
preened in a suit and tie, "Julius D. Eastman in concert"
at St. Augustine Presbyterian Church, The Bronx, July 29, 1962,
and I'm your youthful self in concert, I'm *Jesu* in a Bach duet,
you've just graduated from Curtis, I went to school near Philadelphia,

my mother, like you, was born in Ithaca, I went there when I was young
and stood in the gorges and now I'm in your music's abyss,
catching the pebbled eighth notes, cradling the low
bass tones and smoothing the stones of a grandeur
I never knew we could possess.

2.

Now you're a diva hoisting a queen
aloft at the laundromat, her ruffles frozen in air,
the pic snapped by your boyfriend,

now R. Nemo is at your side on a city block,
two sexy men in sweatshirts at the altar of
a one-way street sign and a church,

R. Nemo Hill the poet, the boy who will later write about you
(I'm a boy, Julius, a boy who will later write about you),

now you're a cowboy with the SEM ensemble, chilling
with Petr Kotik and the dudes, now you're poised at a piano,
now three pianos unfold horizontally, refract diabolically

from yours, now you're a mirror of pianos, now you're a devil,
now you're a star, now you're my star, now I'm yours.

3.

You say you don't want money but *spiritual meat*, you like
the fuck-if-I-care punk of Patti Smith, and reading *Just Kids*
I again inhabit your era—like her, I worked at the Strand,

hauling overstock onto the shelving carts of history,
which are jumbled, improvised, and cluttered as a poem—

Your music, Julius: cascade of coins strewn into a wishing fountain,
St. Joan leading the army into Reims, into New York, into America :: five
          [they count my till at the cash register]   and six
[not money, you say, *spiritual meat*]   and seven ::

4.

I'm unaccountably sad in June and there's a ten-foot disco ball
in the plaza, gussied up for a silent disco. Josh and I are just two
of hundreds at David Geffen Hall as the trumpeters assemble

an invocation: medieval sonorities into free jazz melisma,
seven players unfurling your *Trumpet* into cloistered air.
Sleepily I wrap myself in your riot and spirit, then

go home and slump into the armchair of my anxieties,
which are so much punier than the nation's griefs,
its floods, its fires, its viral weather—

5.

Let me pray for you, Julius. Let me embark
on a pilgrimage to your archives in Buffalo,
let me stand on the edge of Niagara Falls and intone
these songs in your memory. *St. Michael said,*
St. Margaret said, St. Catherine said: JOAN, speak boldly.
Let angels flock from the clouds to join in concert.

Archival

The linen's a dull brown, like a sparrow's head;
it's smeared with sparrow song—triplets of yellow
paint, a salmon's pink, the blue pastel of a cloud-
less sky, the varnished green of spearmint. "So,"

says my grandma, "let's take this down and put it
below the desk," and I remove the thumbtacks,
themselves smeared with paint; we take it, set it
down, careful not to let the fabric curl back.

Across the room your music spirals from
the radio, *World of Echo*, *Unjust Malaise*,
and in another time, Arthur, your thumb's
poised beneath the fingerboard, then flies

thoughtlessly, not requiring thought,
and this time, Julius, your baritone can't
fail, it sails skyward, jumps haughtily
across octaves, and as the cloth slants

downward your voices climb through
her studio, and as we roll up the fabric
in paper and plastic, archival tape, you
fly in as well, into her sparrow's music.

Deep Listening and Other Songs

after Pauline Oliveros

1. Oliveros

I have not been listening deeply to deep listening
I have not been listening sleepily to sleep listening Sleep listens
to me it is a depth   I have yet to sleep
          Screen listens to me   electronic malaise
cistern of bright and byte and sight me lying
                    sprawled
in the tritone   interval of an expanded accordion
                    expand   -ed instru   -meant system
          trombone's vox   amplifying in   cistern digital
     delay   tracking circles into the future field
of   my   ear   poem silent
as the nonsound of my laptop   my brother builds a
                    coliseum

          outside my city on the seven hills   of Rome
my brother the captain of a gladiator crew
          flies his ship through
the prayer-poem   out of space   I mean outer space
colossal ocean beneath the surface of Mars

          trillions of water molecules ring silently a deep
sleep seep see a drone so constant it is silent
                    see a boy so floating he is drowning

2. Or is love—

Deep listening my lover's breathing
          the bed the wishes outside the window whooshing
the twenty-eighth floor of a brain   synapsed staircase
                    concrete gray matter the nothingness
at the bottom of the trash chute the very real somethingness next
          to me is you we're a poem walking through
the Brooklyn Botanical Gardens this rose is named pure poetry
inevitably it wilts
                    though that's not very romantic is it
teasing touch as we wander the cherry
                                        blossom esplanade

I feel like I'm in a Seurat you say
this isn't
love yet but maybe it's an anagram
of something love will turn out to be

3. O Rose LIV

The fifty-fourth rose in the summer palace of the third King of Prussia
doesn't exist   Sanssouci had no roses only queers
Frederick the Great was gay?   I want to remember him
as such
deep listening to the scrotal folds of this rose   eros
the riddle fugue old Bach wrote for little Freddy
an improvisation on the royal theme

[minor triad   leaping down
a drastic seventh curving
chromatic descent   ]

courtly listening
velvet viol and prettified flute
the way classical sound
becomes deep in terms
of age in slippage
of culture the chapel
hall the riddle of
how to play the fugue
Let the King's fortunes grow with the lengthening notes

4. Or so live

Like you listen deeply to whatever and however
I'm all in favor of ambience say what
does deep listening   even mean
at this point I'm just riffing   listening
is a kind of improv   a riff on the river
Pauline I'm trying to walk with the song
into a new place
I'm trying to see the sister cistern of the poem
his brother and their husband and the polyamorous
echoes of myself trying not to wither
if I'm a rose in need of love and water
if I'm a poem in need of sound
boy need of breath   across centuries the way Mitski

becomes deep when me and my husband are doing better
or worse in this lifetime,
for this lifetime
I want to do better
I want to be the husband of the song

Notes

These poems revolve around the work of many artists, musicians, and writers, especially the music of Arthur Russell (1951-1992) and Julius Eastman (1940-1990).

"Self-Portrait as the Cowboy in a Mitski Song" echoes Mitski's 2018 album *Be the Cowboy.*

"Jellyfish": the line "now I find desire imbues it" is from Arthur Russell's song "Sharper Eyes."

"The Clapping Lights" quotes Russell's songs "The Name of the Next Song" and "This Is How We Walk on the Moon."

"Euphoria": The line "the angels opening up heaven . . . Should we say euphoria?" is Julius Eastman's description of the piece.

"Re: Timothée Chalamet Staring Off Into the Distance as Sufjan Stevens Plays Moody Indie Shit at the End of *Call Me by Your Name*" responds to Stevens' "Visions of Gideon" and Luca Guadagnino's 2017 film.

"Smear in the Shape of a Crescent Moon…": *Fagottkonzerte* is German for "bassoon concertos."

"I Put on Julius Eastman": "Why don't you make me feel like a real woman?" are the only lyrics in Eastman's piece *Praise God From Whom All Devils Grow.*

"Everything You Find Goes Back to the Sea": The line "Anything you find goes back to the sea" is from Arthur Russell's song "Canvas Home."

"Winter Sun": The line "tone bone kone" is from Arthur Russell's song of the same title.

"Gigue": Anner Bylsma was renowned for interpreting Johann Sebastian Bach's cello suites on period instruments and using Baroque style; Pablo Casals was one of the first cellists to record the cello suites in 1939.

"Year Year": The tweet referenced is by journalist Prem Thakker.

"The Lord Giveth…": The title, lyrics, and quotes are from a conversation between Eastman and David Garland on Garland's 1984 *Spinning on Air* podcast: https://spinningonair.org/episode-2-julius-eastman/.

"The Vita of St. Valentine": the title refers to the medieval practice of writing saints' lives, or biographies. *Medicus* is Latin for "doctor," and a *consul suffectus* was a temporary replacement for a consul who resigned his post midway through the year. The *Horti Lucullani* refers to the Gardens of Lucullus in Rome, and "herba militaris" means military herb, a nickname for yarrow.

"Orchid": the first line alludes to a quote from Walter Benjamin: "The sight of immediate reality has become an orchid in the land of technology," in "The Work of Art in the Age of Mechanical Reproduction," *Illuminations* (Mariner Books, 2019), trans. by Harry Zohn and ed. by Hannah Arendt.

"Fame": The line "it's my world, it's my song" quotes Arthur Russell's "I Couldn't Say It to Your Face."

"Arthur, 1992": The line "being sad is not a crime" is from Arthur Russell's song "Love Comes Back."

"*Joy Boy* at the Branded Saloon" is after a performance of Julius Eastman's "Joy Boy" by the ensemble ChamberQUEER, alongside Baroque music and an instrumental "chorale" by Kebra Seyoun-Charles.

"On the Sixth Anniversary of Pulse": The line "a mighty fortress is our god" is the title of a Lutheran chorale whose melody Julius Eastman quoted in *Gay Guerrilla*. Eastman's phrase "Right thought right speech right action right music" was inspired by the Noble Eightfold Path in Buddhism.

"Music for a Queer Pastoral": The Jacques J. Rancourt poem quoted is "Western Wall."

"Music for a Queer Conservator": The italics are from Julius Eastman's piece *Prelude to The Holy Presence of Joan D'Arc.*

"Deep Listening and Other Songs": "Let the King's fortune grow with the lengthening notes" is a loose translation of the Latin phrase *Notulis crescentibus crescat Fortuna Regis*, which accompanies the

Canon a 2 per Augmentationem, contrario Motu in Bach's *Musical Offering*, dedicated to Frederick II of Prussia.

Composer Pauline Oliveros's practice of deep listening is, in her words, "a way of listening in every possible way to everything possible, to hear no matter what you are doing"; more information can be found through the Center for Deep Listening, https://www.deeplistening.rpi.edu/.

Over the past couple decades, scholars and musicians have done excellent work remixing and reinterpreting Russell and Eastman. Here are a few places to start:

Ndikung, Bonaventure Soh Bejeng, et al. *We Have Delivered Ourselves from the Tonal: Of, towards, on, for Julius Eastman*. SAVVY Contemporary in collaboration with Archive Books, 2020.

King, Richard. *Travels Over Feeling: Arthur Russell, a Life*. Anthology Editions, 2024.

Lawrence, Tim. *Hold On to Your Dreams: Arthur Russell and the Downtown Music Scene*. Duke University Press, 2009.

Levine Packer, Reneé, and Mary Jane Leach. *Gay Guerrilla: Julius Eastman and His Music*. Boydell and Brewer, 2015.

Marble, Matt. *Buddhist Bubblegum: Esotericism in the Creative Process of Arthur Russell*. Coolgrove Press, 2021.

Wild Combination: A Portrait of Arthur Russell. Directed by Matt Wolf, Polari Pictures, 2008.

Acknowledgments

Many thanks to the following journals and their editors for publishing poems from this manuscript, sometimes in earlier versions:

Afternoon Visitor: "Sonnet"
Alien Magazine: "Music for a Queer Pastoral"
And Change: "*Illustrations for Fourteen Poems by C.P. Cavafy*"
Baltimore Review: "Arthur, 1992"
Blue Bag Press: "In the Third Year"
Denver Quarterly: "Endearing tunes :: ear ending unset"
Dialogist: "Jellyfish"
exquisites vol. 5: "Enharmonic"
Fairy Tale Review: "Dear Dear"
Ghost Harmonics: *Oscillations*: "Deep Listening and Other Songs"
The Journal: "Eli"
Moist Poetry Journal: "Another Thought"
Only Poems: "*Portrait of an Artist (Pool with Two Figures)*," "Jews Against Genocide"
petrichor: "Encaustic," "Give," "Bevel"
Prelude: "Ambient Gay Cortical Jenga"
Quarter Notes: "*Joy Boy* at the Branded Saloon"
Rejection Letters: "Re: Timothée Chalamet Staring Off Into the Distance as Sufjan Stevens Plays Moody Indie Shit at the End of Call Me by Your Name"
Salamander: "I Put on Julius Eastman"
Shō Poetry Journal: "Self-Portrait as the Cowboy in a Mitski Song," "Fear Fear"
South Dakota Review: "Everything You Find Goes Back to the Sea"
Waltz: "Birthday Poem," "Orchid"

Some of these poems appeared in a chapbook, *Feedback Harmonies*, from Seven Kitchens Press in 2024.

The composer Hannah Cai Sobel set "Jellyfish" for soprano and string quartet and wrote a string quartet inspired by "Your Melodies."

~

This book would not be possible without the generosity and support of many friends, writers, musicians, and teachers.

To Chris Hood, Christine Leja, Will Fisher, and all my high school English teachers: thanks for encouraging me early on in my poetic journey. Many thanks also to Christy Payne and all high school librarians!

To Nat Anderson, who saw the first poems in this manuscript: I'm so grateful to have studied with you, and for your insight and care. I'm also grateful to Peter Schmidt, Betsy Bolton, and to the Swarthmore English Department as a whole for the Morrell-Potter Summer Stipend.

To Jamie Blasina, Clara Rottsolk, and the Swarthmore Music Department: thanks for your instruction in music and voice.

To Donna Fournier: thanks for your library mentorship, and for helping me find live Arthur Russell recordings through *DRAM* in summer 2020.

To Hannah Cai Sobel: may all the eggs land in your basket. Thank you for the love, the laughter, and the music.

To Nicole Liu and Cat Crochunis-Brown: who are not only close friends but great writers and thoughtful readers, I'm very grateful for our phone calls and poetry talk.

To my dear friends, who were early readers of some of these poems: thank you, and much love. Thanks especially to Daniel Barnum, Kathryn Bratt-Pfotenhauer, Lonely Christopher, Chris Campanioni, Joshua Garcia, Sean Glatch, Kieran Huang, Rahul Sen, Jimin Seo, Fern Trujillo, Stu Watson, and Evan Williams.

To Michael Broder, David Roderick, Janeen Armstrong, and Rebecca Lehmann: thanks for providing mentorship and guidance as I've made my way in the poetry world.

To my colleagues at SNFL: I'm so grateful to work with such smart, kind, creative people.

To Tom Lee and Steve Knutson: infinite thanks for sharing Arthur's music with us, and for allowing me to quote his music here.

To Ron Mohring: thanks for your care in making the chap and for your stewardship of queer poetry.

To Randall Mann: a thousand thanks for believing in this book and for selecting it for the Louise Bogan Award. Thanks also for the generous citation.

To Jessica Cuello and Richie Hofmann for their illuminating blurbs: thank you, thank you, thank you.

To the entire team at Trio House, especially Kris Bigalk, Joel Coggins, and Natasha Kane: thanks so much for all your hard work shepherding this book from pdf to physical object. It means the world. I'm so thrilled to be part of the Trio House family.

To David Groff and Samantha Hernandez: I couldn't ask for better editors. Thank you for your dedicated and thoughtful work on *Dear Dear*. You made the manuscript into a fuller version of itself.

To Mira, Drew, Levi, Mieke, Michael, and Paco: I love you deeply and am so grateful for you all.

And to you, dear reader, thank you.

About the Author

Reuben Gelley Newman is a writer, librarian, and musician based in Brooklyn, NY. He is the author of the chapbook *Feedback Harmonies* (Seven Kitchens Press, 2024), and his poems have appeared in *Denver Quarterly*, *Fairy Tale Review*, *Fence*, *Ninth Letter*, *Only Poems*, and *Salamander*. A former intern at Copper Canyon Press, he has edited for *The Adroit Journal* and *Couplet Poetry*. His reviews have appeared in *Adroit*, *The Brooklyn Rail*, and *Diode*. He holds an MS in Library and Information Science from University at Buffalo and a BA in English Literature from Swarthmore College.

About the Book

Dear Dear was designed at Trio House Press through the collaboration of:

David Groff, Lead Editor
Samantha Hernandez, Supporting Editor
Natasha Kane, Interior Designer
Joel W. Coggins, Cover Designer

The text is set in Adobe Caslon Pro.

About the Press

Trio House Press is an independent nonprofit press based in Minneapolis, Minnesota. We publish poetry and prose that moves, inspires, and encourages connection, empathy, and understanding, with a special emphasis on underrepresented voices and topics. To find out more about Trio House Press, please visit our website at http://www.triohousepress.org.

www.ingramcontent.com/pod-product-compliance
Lightning Source LLC
LaVergne TN
LVHW090953270626
842129LV00032B/456

* 9 7 8 1 9 4 9 4 8 7 6 6 4 *